darkling
/ˈdɑːklɪŋ/
adjective
growing dark or characterised by darkness

DARKLING

An Advent Journey

Gideon Heugh

Copyright © 2022 by Gideon Heugh
All rights reserved

ISBN: 9798438105817

All Bible quotations are World English Bible

For the people living in darkness

CONTENTS

Introduction 1

How to use this book 5

An Invocation for Advent 7

I · Seeing in the Dark

Dark matter 10

Seeing in the dark 12

Speechless 14

Miracles and tragedies 16

The radiant void 18

Questions for reflection 20

II · The Dark Body of God

The bells of Evensong 22

The dark body of God 24

Lamp 26

Dark matter (two) 28

Radical 30

Questions for reflection 32

III · Liturgies of Loss

Two benedictions for grief 34

Disaster 36

Eternity's shore 38

(Don't) keep calm and carry on 40

Giving shape to our grief 42

Questions for reflection 44

IV · The Fecund Fallow

The fecund fallow 46

Sabbath 48

The small things 50

Creatures of the in-between 52

Lessons from my suckiness 54

Questions for reflection 56

V · O Holy Night

Firmament 58

Hope as planetary motion 60

When there is no room at the inn 62

Where the stars lead us 64

Questions for reflection 66

Coda · The Flesh of the World

The flesh of the world 68

About the author 73

DARKLING

*Stare into the sun and it will blind you.
Not so the dark.
Un-shield yourself from the night
and over time you will start to see;
your senses will sharpen; your heart open
as it follows the stars—
whose meaning only now are you beginning to grasp.*

Introduction

We live in darkling days.

We are far from the first. We will not be the last. But this season of gathering night is ours. This heaviness is the one that we are ordained to carry—here, now, two decades deep into the twenty-first century.

It is not yet a darkness that we can understand. How do we come to terms with a global pandemic? With the existential threat of the climate emergency? Or with the mass theft of our attention by tech companies? How do we make a map of the growing tide of loneliness, depression and anxiety? Or the increasingly polarised and too-frequently angry realm of political and social discourse?

It is not always possible to know what you are going through until you have gone through it. Perhaps only history will know what to make of these times.

We live in darkling days.
So how should we respond?

In our culture, darkness and night are metaphors that are charged with negativity. They are synonyms for evil, terror, despair. The darkling things of life are to be shunned. Feared, even.

We see this in our culture's preference towards 'spring' energy. We want growth and renewal and movement. To stay where you are is to fall behind. We want to climb, to strive, to accumulate, and to do this all the time. We have forgotten that there is a season for everything—even the dark.

To live life in all its fullness, we need to find and cultivate the spirit of autumn and winter within us. We need to learn to live with the dark, not try and blast it away with neon lights and toxic positivity.

Advent is an ideal time to do this. Or at least, it should be. In recent times it has been swallowed by Christmas—becoming a countdown for the big event rather than an event itself. Advent these days is synonymous with chocolate-filled calendars, and little else. Yet once upon a time Advent and Christmas were two distinct seasons. Christmas was the time for celebration. Serious celebration—it was a twelve day feast! Advent, on the other hand, was a time for reflection, recognition, and anticipation.

Advent is not about the bright glare of festivity; it is about the lonely, flickering candle. It is a time to reflect, to slow our pace, and to hunker down while the cold winds blow. During Advent, we do not beat back the darkness. We acknowledge it. We wait within it. We listen to what it has to say. We do not fight the lengthening nights—we welcome them.

So, this Advent: we reflect on our hopes... and our fears. We look back at what has gone well in our lives... and what has not. We stop to gaze at our own souls. A wound that is never examined is a wound that is never healed. So we recognise the darkness. We acknowledge how hard things have been. We accept that life is this sacred mix of the bitter and the beautiful, and that often there is less of a gap between those two than we might think.

And, we anticipate. Because even if things really are all doom and gloom, they will not always be. Because although we recognise and acknowledge the heavy realities, we also recognise and acknowledge that, at any moment, something new may be born.

We live in darkling days. Okay. Let us see what we might find in them.

God of darkness,
Spirit of winter,
Angels of the long night—
grant us the strength of vulnerability;
help us to dwell in the places of waiting;
help us to listen to what the shadows are saying.
Amen.

Gideon Heugh, November 2022

How to use this book

Different Christian denominations vary in their precise definition of when Advent is. To keep things simple, the devotions in this book run from December 1 to December 24, with a little extra something before and after. But don't worry about sticking to the exact dates. It can be dipped in and out of, or read in one big gulp. I have written the book either to be used for personal reflection, or in a group setting. The devotions are divided into five parts, with discussion questions at the end of each section. Each devotion ends with a short blessing, prayer, or prompt. Feel free to sit with these for a while. I love the spiritual intentionality that seasons such as Advent can create, so let's lean into it. Make it a daily ritual. Wrap yourself in the darkling pages.

Prelude
An Invocation for Advent

Welcome, stranger. Come in. Lay down.
Let us remove this burden of light
that you have carried around for too long.

It is not the darkness that has blinded you.

But now, free from the glare,
you can let your eyes adjust.
Now, sheltered from all that knowing,
you can sit within the shadows' strange conferring.
Together we will light a candle—
not to vanquish the dark,
but to further articulate it.

Here may you find the wisdom of winter.
Here may you unlearn the folly of a life
that always climbs the mountain,
that believes in accumulation,
that does not join God as she too lies fallow—
as she too opens herself
to absence.

Part I

SEEING IN THE DARK

'I will give you the treasures of darkness and hidden riches of secret places, that you may know that it is I, Yahweh, who calls you by your name.'
—Isaiah 45:3

December 1
Dark matter

Do not show me your bright stars;
we cannot grow
among the shine and the glitter;

show me instead your dark matter,
lead me to the places
where those stars collapsed;

let's fall towards the blackness together,
across the event horizon
into something better.

* * *

How often do you show the world the real you?

We all wear masks. We all say 'I'm fine' even when we are not. We all filter our image so it looks as though we have got everything together.

Yet there is so much power in simply being who we are. Our pain, our imperfections, our inglorious pasts—these are all part of us, and we are stunning regardless.

If we hide from these things, if we filter them or cover them up, they will eventually consume us. But if we have the audacity to be vulnerable, to trust, to be our authentic and shattered selves, we might discover the infinite grace that is available to us.

We are all making it up as we go along. We are all fighting a battle of some kind. And it is from these cracks in our wounded hearts that love can flow in—and out.

God of dark matter,
Grant us the audacity to be vulnerable. Help us to see and accept our stunning enough-ness; and let the grace and love flow.
Amen.

December 2
Seeing in the dark

Most of us have no idea how well a human being can see in the dark.

That is because we are rarely exposed to darkness for long. We switch on a light. We flick on a torch. The night sky is forever illuminated by a neon glare.

When I was young, my family would go camping together a lot. My father would tell me that, on a clear night, you would see better if you avoided artificial light. You needed to let your eyes adjust.

This requires patience—it takes about 30 minutes for the human eye to fully adjust to darkness. But when it does, you will be astonished by how much you can see.

A torch can only show you what is within its field of view. And if it goes out, you are in trouble. But let your eyes become accustomed to a low level of light, and you will see far more.

In the difficult times of life—the darkling times; the days of uncertainty, sadness, heartache, loss—often we just want to turn on the light.

We want the easy answer.
The immediate healing.
The miraculous breakthrough.

It rarely comes.

Perhaps we would be better off sitting in the darkness. Perhaps we would be better off letting our eyes adjust.

Who knows, then, what we might be able to see?

God of night-sight,
Help us to not be drawn too quickly to artificial lights. Give us the courage to wait with you in the dark. Help our eyes to adjust to these darkling days. Amen.

December 3
Speechless

I am going to begin this reflection on one of the perils of social media with a quote that I saw on social media: 'Are you saying something because you feel as though you have to say something, or because you have something to say?'

This challenged me. In Social Media Land, we are encouraged to immediately give our reaction to everything. Nuance and deep thought are evacuated: anything can (and should) be interpreted in a short, snappy statement.

But the world is complicated. Issues are complicated. Mystery surrounds and permeates much.

What if we returned to a counter-cultural mindset in which we 'dwelt' on things—in which we set up camp in an idea and looked around? What if we gave ourselves and others space, and stopped defining success in terms of instant reaction?

We should normalise saying 'I don't know', or even nothing at all. If we do discuss something, we should not be afraid of talking (and listening!) at length, and in detail.

We do not have all the answers. Nor do we need to. Great wonder and beauty often leave us speechless. A star-strewn night is its own soliloquy. Let us treat that as a lesson.

May we not give an answer if we do not yet have a good one. May we ponder the mysteries in our own hearts. May we refuse to simplify complexity. May we give space to ideas, to people, to ourselves. And may we see the reflection of the stars in the deep waters; and not have a clue what to say.

December 4
Miracles and tragedies

Dreams really do come true. Except when they don't.

You can achieve anything you set your mind to. Except when you can't.

Miracles happen all the time… and so do tragedies.

Some things will turn out better than expected. Some things will turn out worse. There will be joy, pleasure, wonder and delight. And there will be grief, agony, anxiety and despair. There will be moments that take your breath away, and there will be moments when it feels as though you can't breathe.

Toxic positivity doesn't help anyone. But neither does cynicism. To be human is to know the bitter and the beautiful, and to accept that they both belong.

Mourning can turn into dancing. Dancing can turn into mourning.

This does not make us love life any less, but love it all the more. It is precious because at any moment it could break. This is the strange interplay that so much art is born from. The painful-precious aches that draw us into the true depth of life.

So we embrace life with everything we have; because of the miracles, and because of the tragedies.

God of dark and light,
Help us to live in the dance of the bitter-beautiful—
the painful-precious. Help us to accept that it all belongs. And help us to find the true depths of life.
Amen.

December 5
The radiant void

Western spirituality is shaped by 'mountain thinking.' It is life as the long trail, with wide vistas from the top giving you a perspective that you otherwise would not see.

But wisdom is less likely to be found at the top of a mountain than it is at the bottom of a pit.

Disappointment. Abandonment. Redundancy. Grief. Heartbreak. Betrayal. We never wish to go through such things. But once we have, we may realise that it is these times that most profoundly shape us.

You can fall into a pit at any time. Unlike climbing a mountain, we may not have a choice in the matter. You can hit the bottom pretty quickly. And it hurts. But, stumbling blindly, painfully through the dark, we can happen upon truths that we otherwise may not have discovered.

At the top of a mountain, you can see so much that it can be hard to know what to focus on. But at the bottom of a pit, everything is stripped down to the gasping real. If there is any wisdom in me, it is not because of anything inherent within me. I have done a lot of stupid things. I still do. If there is any depth to me, it is because I have been to the deep. It is not because I have climbed a lot of mountains, but because I have fallen into a lot of pits.

The descent into an underworld is such a common trope in mythology that the Greeks had a specific name for it: *katabasis*. It essentially means 'a descent made to gain understanding.' In so many myths, the protagonists must make both a literal and figurative journey into the dark in order to find what they need to complete their quest.

It is not a glittering ascent; it is encountering the void, and discovering that the darkness too can be radiant.

Whatever deadly dark you are going through, may you find your way to the other side. May you know the divine presence there in the midst of it. May you find healing, rebirth, and understanding.

Seeing in the Dark—questions for reflection:

1. Do you feel able to show the world the real you? Does it matter if you do not?

2. What are some of the 'easy' answers that we can be drawn to, when the truth might be a little bit more complicated?

3. Do you ever feel pressured to say something just for the sake of it? How can we cultivate practices of speechlessness?

4. 'Life is precious because at any moment it could break.' Is this true? If it is, then why?

5. What truths have you learned during the dark periods of your life?

Part II

THE DARK BODY OF GOD

'Behold, God is great, and we do not know him.'
—Job 36:26

December 6
The bells of Evensong

If I lay still for long enough
I can hear the faintest echo
of the bells of evensong.

Deep in the long past
I walk through wide church doors
and into candlelight;
there I find a seat
next to the Holy Ghost, who is always
so quiet. She likes to listen
to the choir, who breathe out rumours
of some heaven,
whose harmonies are the best kind of sermon.

Now I walk into church
and all the lights are fluorescent
and everyone is shouting out answers
instead of listening
for a better question.

I do not see the Holy Ghost.

I wonder if she, like the bells of Evensong,
is slowly fading into whatever it is
that was once a memory.

* * *

There is something about choral Evensong that resonates powerfully with me. And it is more than just the beautiful, haunting music. It is the silences. The pauses. The gaps. And, in winter, the candlelight.

Candlelight has a unique quality. It does not extinguish darkness; it helps to articulate it.

Everyone has their preferred styles of worship. Which is as it should be. But if we do not create space for silence, reverence, beauty—and for a quality of light that gives voice to the shadows, rather than crowds them out—then we are missing something vital.

Try making a practice this Advent of lighting a candle. Even if it is just for one evening. Turn off all other lights. Take a few moments to be still; quiet. Breathe. Listen. Be.

December 7
The dark body of God

The Big Bang—the moment when the universe came into being—is usually depicted as an explosion of light. But there is a problem with this: it would not have appeared to be light at all.

The energy involved would have created a huge amount of light radiation, but the density of the universe meant that the light was 'trapped' (I don't really understand either, but roll with it). A few hundred thousand years would have passed after the Big Bang before any light was visible. And even after that, given that there were no stars yet (the first ones were born when the universe was around 100 million years old) the universe would have remained a pretty dark place.

In the book of Genesis, darkness comes first too. Light had to be created, but the darkness was already there. Spirit is described as hovering over the dark waters (Genesis 1:2). It is from here that creation comes. Darkness is not contrary to creation. It is part of it.

Like the Big Bang, God is often described as a brilliant light. But not always. At least, not in the Hebrew Bible: when Abram has a vision of God in his sleep, it is said that 'great darkness fell on him' (Genesis 15:12). Moses is described as approaching 'the thick darkness where God was' (Exodus 20:21). And the psalmist says of God that 'thick darkness was under his feet... He made darkness his hiding place... darkness of waters, thick clouds of the skies.' (Psalm 18:9,11)

A whole book, Job, is dedicated to God being unknowable. Time and again throughout scripture, the divine voice refuses to give answers. Time and again, we walk in the dark. Maybe that is not such a bad thing. Maybe that is where creation takes place. That is where beginnings happen. That is where we find the divine body—looming large in the blackness.

Think of the dark waters in your own life. What if the Holy Spirit was hovering above them?

December 8
Lamp

'Your word is a lamp to my feet, and a light for my path.' (Psalm 119:105)

Sounds nice, doesn't it? But the thing about a lamp is that it will only illuminate a few steps in front of you. It guides you through, rather than eliminates, the darkness.

We long to see the whole path. But the darkling divine tells us: just take the next step. The path is there, even if all you can see is your feet.

I am sure that there will have been plenty of times in your life where you could not see a way ahead, and yet just by moving forward, the way was made.

It reminds me of the early days of the coronavirus pandemic. We had no idea what was ahead. No one did. It was hard. Very hard. For many, it still is. But we are here nonetheless.

We got through, and are getting through, simply by putting one foot in front of the other.

May the shimmer of the divine fall about your feet. May you know that there is a path, even when you cannot see it. May you have the strength to take the next step—even if the next step means holding still, and waiting to see what comes wandering through.

December 9
Dark matter (two)

There is something that you might not have noticed about the universe. Which is that most of it—80 per cent in fact—is missing. And we have no idea where it is.

By observing the motion of stars, scientists can estimate how much mass there is in the universe. And all of the things we can see—planets, stars, nebulae, galaxies—does not add up to what *should* be there.

Something is having a huge gravitational effect on the universe, and we have no idea what it is. This missing mass is known as dark matter. You may remember it showing up on December 1.

Think about the things that have the biggest effect on our lives. These are often the things we would prefer not to see. The things we would rather ignore. The things we hide away.

Pain. Loss. Failure. Heartbreak. The dark matter.

In our culture, we prefer not to put these things on display. We would much sooner lock our pulped hearts away than wear them on our sleeves.

But a worldview that ignores the dark matter is ignoring most of the world.

That is what is so stunning and necessary about the Christ story. A god-figure tortured and executed. Divinity wounded and broken and vulnerable. God-as-weakness. God-as-dark-matter.

We cannot ignore brokenness or shove it into the hidden corners of our universe. Hurt that is unaddressed will unravel us. We must acknowledge, accept, and step into the darkness. Only then might we find that resurrection is waiting on the other side.

God of weakness,
Thank you that you do not shy away from the brokenness. Thank you that you are there in the midst of the night. Let us know your closeness as we step into the dark matter.
Amen.

December 10
Radical

There have been times over the last few years that I have caught myself sliding into cynicism. It is all too easy in these darkling days—when the world is so obviously not as it ought to be; when injustice seems to be everywhere. But to respond to darkness by closing the gate of our hearts is a failure of imagination. In the eye of Spirit is the roguish glint of possibility.

Are you fed up with the way the world is? Good. Roll up your sleeves: there's work to be done. True humanity does not put up walls—it draws close to the pain. Hope does not ignore the darkness; it swallows it up, using it as fuel that we might burn all the brighter. We are broken so that we might give back a fiercer and more inclusive love—a love that says 'I know.'

Piety does not look like docility. It is a ragged, dogged, dreadfully felt thing. It is the psalmist smashing together hope and despair at the bottom of a bone-lined pit. It is the prophet hammering at the walls of the temple, shouting until their throat bleeds that God despises religion—that her cold fury is set against those who allow injustice to exist. It is the woman wiping tears and priceless perfume on the feet of the rabbi—the rabbi who taught that it is not the rich or powerful who are blessed; that love does not look like comfort.

Piety is not a grand procession through a gilded church. It is a group of dreamers huddled in a small room, bold, dangerously vulnerable, trading whispers of resistance. The pious are radicals. Radical in both senses of the word: 'advocating or based on thorough or complete political or social change,' and 'relating to or affecting the fundamental nature of something; far-reaching or thorough.' Radical literally means *forming the root* (think radish). The pious plant themselves in the things that matter; they are rooted in justice, mercy, and a wild each-otherness. They walk humbly, but relentlessly.

May you be radical. May you believe in and pursue change. And may you be rooted in the depths of life.

The Dark Body of God—questions for reflection:

1. If you have one, what is your preferred style of worship? How could you make more space in your spiritual life for silence, reverence, and beauty?

2. Has there been a moment in your life when new creation has come unexpectedly out of dark times?

3. Name the times when you have not seen the whole path ahead, but were able to take the next step. Is there anything going on in your life now that you could apply this to?

4. What is the 'dark matter' in your life that you would prefer not to see? How might you be able to better acknowledge and accept it?

5. What does it mean to be rooted, and how can this help us to avoid cynicism?

Part III

LITURGIES OF LOSS

'Jesus wept.'
—John 11:35

December 11
Two benedictions for grief

If we wished for a lighter life,
It would be a life without love.
Spirit, be with me as I carry this weight.

If we wished for an unbroken life,
It would be a life without love.
Spirit, be with me as I carry these wounds.

If we wished for an uncomplicated life,
It would be a life without love.
Spirit, be with as I carry this pain.

We mourn those we have lost. We give thanks for their lives. We remember them. We hold them now. We hold the weight of grief; we hold the wounds; we hold the pain; and above all; and above all; and above all; we hold the love.

Amen.

May we grow in awareness of our grief;
may we listen to it and learn its name.
Let no one say that it must be hidden;
let no one say that we must be ashamed.

May we grow in awareness of our grief;
may we know that we need not face it alone.
Let all have the nearness or space that they need;
let all have the opportunity to be known.

May we grow in awareness of our grief;
may we weep, and weep, and weep.
Let us know that sorrow is the tenacity of love;
only love can lift so high—or pierce so deep.

December 12
Disaster

Disaster. From the Latin *Dis-astrum*.
Dis—negation. *Astrum*—stars.

A disaster is when you are voided of the stars; when you lose sight of the heavens; when you are untethered from the firmament.

What do those stars represent?

Something that guides us. Something that lights us. Something upon which we can always depend.
You will know what the stars of your life are.

A disaster is the loss of that which orientates us. We become dizzied; overwhelmed; uncertain.

Without our stars we feel lost.

How many disasters have we collectively faced over the last few years? How many have you faced in your own life?

You should not be shocked to feel the way you do.

The first step back towards life is to name what we are experiencing.

Beloved, you have been de-starred.

God of the skies,
We call out in our starless night.
Be with us in our lost-ness.
Draw close as we name our disasters.
Amen.

December 13
Eternity's shore

When I was in my early 20s, there was a Christian worship song that would leave me convulsed with weeping. The first lines of the final verse go: 'When we arrive at eternity's shore / Where death is just a memory and tears are no more.'

It is beautifully written. The reason it resonated so powerfully with me was because I was deeply depressed. Life felt unbearable, and I wanted to escape. The idea of reaching a place where tears were no more left me utterly overwhelmed with longing and grief—desperate to be rid of my loneliness and pain.

My faith is very different now, and there are few worship songs that I still feel comfortable singing. Life can still feel unbearable. There is still great pain. But now I am not so desperate for the elsewhere heaven. Now I pour my life into looking to the heaven that is here.

Wendell Berry said that 'A creed and a grave never did equal the life of anything.' Friedrich Nietzsche said that if you do not find eternity here, you are probably not going to find it anywhere else.

And in the Bible, in the book of Genesis, the voice of God declares again and again that *this world* is good.

There are times when I still want to escape. But then I play a silly game with my daughter. Or dance. Or listen to the dawn chorus. Or watch a sunset. Or play football. Or eat some really good food. Or go to the pub with friends. Or read a poem. Or listen to Bach. Or listen to Britney. Or have sex. Or eat an apple. Or laugh at a great joke. Or go for a run. Or watch *Lord of the Rings*. Or bake bread. Or play video games with friends. Or do yoga. Or smell a rose.

Do something that is here. Something that is life. Because heaven is here. Heaven is life. It is good. And it is unbearable. It is unbearable. And it is good.

Make your own list of things that ground you in this world. Things that are here, now, that fill your cup.

December 14
(Don't) keep calm and carry on

In Jesus' time, as soon as someone was given the news about the death of a loved one, they would have torn their clothing.

It is still a custom among traditional Jewish communities today. It is known as *kriah*—an outward symbol of grief; the rending of a garment echoing the rending of the soul.

In modern British culture, the words 'keep calm and carry on' have become something of a national mantra. Originating on posters that were put up during the bombing raids of World War Two, you will now find it printed on mugs and beer mats as a symbol of our supposed stiff-upper-lip-ness.

Such stoicism can be admirable. Sometimes it can be necessary. But it can also be damaging.

Wounds must be allowed to speak.

If it is too much to keep calm and carry on, then don't. If grief feels like you are being torn to pieces, then be torn to pieces.

The healing will come, eventually, but not if we show a stiff upper lip to that which must be healed.
You cannot process what you do not express.

God of our wounds,
Help me to be unafraid to make my kriah.
Help me to let my wounds speak.
Help me to see that the first step to healing
can be tearing.
Amen.

December 15
Giving shape to our grief

In Western culture, we have little that gives shape to our grief. The unwritten rule of sorrow, it often can seem, is that it is best kept at bay. Not so with *shiva*.

Shiva is the Hebrew word for seven. It also refers to a ritualised week-long period of mourning. The purpose of the shiva week, which takes place after the funeral of a loved one, is to give those grieving the space and time to begin to process their loss. It is a guide to help bring you through what cannot be navigated.

When you are visiting someone who is sitting shiva, you are not allowed to speak until the bereaved speaks. While this seems odd, there is a good reason behind it: the person who is bereaved may not want to talk. Or you may end up saying something that makes them feel worse, not better. There are some things that no words can bring comfort to. Often, we feel as though we need to say something to those who are struggling—merely for the sake of saying something. But presence is more meaningful than platitudes.

For the duration of the shiva week, mourners will stay in their home, or the home of the loved one who has passed away. Traditionally, they will sit on low chairs: a physical representation of a desolate spirit.

Shiva confronts you with your broken reality. If your heart is crushed, then there is no sense in pretending otherwise. If you are depressed, then it is no good saying 'I'm fine.' At times of great sorrow, you cannot simply continue to live as normal.

After my grandmother died, a group of people from the synagogue near to where she grew up came to her funeral. They did not know our family, but they wanted to do everything to ensure that our sorrow wasn't endured alone. In shiva, the community comes together to care for the mourners. They do whatever they can to meet the needs of the bereaved—from preparing meals to saying prayers.

May we reach out in our darkling days, and may we allow ourselves to be reached.

Liturgies of Loss—questions for reflection:

1. 'If we wished for an unbroken life, it would be a life without love.' What does this statement mean to you?

2. What have been some of the 'stars'—the things that orientate you—that you have lost?

3. Where can we find the eternity in our everyday lives?

4. Are there any wounds that you have not allowed to speak?

5. What are the ways in which you can give shape to your grief?

Part IV

THE FECUND
FALLOW

'But the seventh year you shall let it rest and lie fallow, that the poor of your people may eat.'
—Exodus 23:11

December 16
The fecund fallow

Fecund: high-yielding; fertile; fruitful; rich.
Fallow: dormant; inactive; idle; slow.

And what if all this waiting;
this trembling body of longing;
this channel of sap's quiet idling;
what if it is here—
not in the crowded upthrusts,
but in the un-looked-for solitudes,
in the mist that makes doubtful the path—
that life at last discovers itself?
What if the fallow has all along been fecund?

Beneath the cold soil,
the roots are discovering
their grit.

* * *

At great cost, our culture has neglected the fallow. There is a relentless call for more, based on a misguided belief that the resources of our planet—and of our souls—have no limits. It is a belief that productivity and progress are the only gods that matter. It is a belief that is destroying us.

Rest is not merely a means to an end. It is an end in and of itself. It is an essential part of our aliveness. There is beauty and life in the wintering times. The ancient Hebrews understood this. Fallow periods were enshrined by law. Ignoring the call to rest was punishable, shockingly, by death. But that is where endless production leads.

God of stillness,
Let us be idle.
Let us wait, slow, pause, rest, hibernate.
Let us find the fecundity in the fallow.
Amen.

December 17
Sabbath

All that noise pervading you—all the scrolling, the browsing, the endless rushing around—no wonder your soul has crawled beneath your bones; no wonder it doesn't want to come out.

Distraction pushes the whispers of your heart outside of your awareness; busyness crowds the space within you until your spirit curls up into a ball.

Yet in stillness you can arrive, slowly, at the gentle truths of yourself. In returning to quietude time after time you can begin to gain the trust of your shy depths.

If you do not make space in your time, then your time will run out of space; your life will over-bleed, spilling out until it loses its form and viscosity.

What has no boundaries has no shape. Create boundaries in your life by deliberately, uncompromisingly creating space for the things that matter most.

This is what Sabbath is all about—making space in time. It is a place for sinking into the depths rather than skimming the surface of life.

Our lives should have a rhythm to them. But this only happens if we put it there. Otherwise we will find our feet are moving faster than our souls can keep up with. We ourselves must create a beautiful cadence. We ourselves must add the pauses, the soft descents, the deep breaths. For how can we learn the gorgeous secrets of our souls if we never stop to listen?

May you make space in time for wonder. May you make space in time for rest. May you make space in time for beauty. May you make space in time for sorrow. May you make space in time for gratitude. May you make space in time for hope. May you create continuums of soulfulness, and let your being breathe.

December 18
The small things

During some of the most difficult periods of my life, it has often been the simple things that have kept me from falling apart. A meal with friends. A walk in the dawn-lit woods. A poem. Birdsong.

Fellowship, art, and food won't heal all our wounds or make everything okay. But they can keep us going. When surrounded by 'big things', falling back on the 'small things' can save us.

The things that heal us are not complicated or expensive. But they are increasingly marginalised.

In our culture, sleep is seen as a luxury, rather than a necessity; food is made to be convenient, rather than nourishing; connection has been outsourced to screens; and busyness and distraction have all but eliminated the ability to dwell in our depths.

It doesn't have to be that way. If a culture Is causing us harm, then we should create our own.

Sometimes pain is just pain. Sometimes sorrow is just sorrow. And there is no explanation or higher plan behind it. We can't rationalise or spiritualise our way through them. But we can live our way through them, with each other, one day at a time.

May fellowship and food always find you. May you know that the small things in life are really the big things. May you find healing in simple pleasures. May good sleep, real food, connection, pleasure, and reflection find you. And may you there be restoration for your body, mind, and soul.

December 19
Creatures of the in-between

Too often we can spend our time waiting for something to happen that will solve our problems. A solution to be imparted. A breakthrough to occur. A dream to be fulfilled.

We can be so desperate to cross that threshold of arrival that we miss what is happening in the in-between. We are so desperate to reach the promised land that we fail to see the life that is held in the wilderness. We are so obsessed with the product that we miss the process.

Life happens at the speed of now. It is happening today, not tomorrow. If we say, 'I'll be happy / enlightened / content when I get [x],' then we will miss life.

We need to learn to be creatures of the in-between—to live in the absolution of the present, not the unforgiving unreality of 'if' and 'then' and 'only' and 'when'. It is easier said than done. Especially during darkling days. But we are where we are, so we might as well look around and see what joys or truths that the 'here' might hold.

Breakthroughs do happen. Dreams do get fulfilled. Sometimes, they do not. In the meantime, life is unfolding, and the invitation is open.

God of the in-between,
Help us to keep our eyes on the here and now.
Help us to dwell full-heartedly in the present.
Help us to see that life has started,
and will not wait for us.
Amen.

December 20
Lessons from my suckiness

I suck at this. Really, I do.

I don't write about all the things I write about because I'm good at them, but the opposite. I'm preaching to myself, and letting you eavesdrop. And that's kind of the point.

I once saw a great quote that said, 'Writers are beggars telling other people where they found bread.' I am very much a beggar. I'm hungry for the food of the soul. I know how much I need it. How pale and shallow life is without it.

I write about being mindful and attentive because I am so easily distracted. I write about nature and movement because so often I am stuck in front of a screen, back sore from too much sitting. I write about peace because I struggle to find any. I write about Sabbath because I am terrible at doing Sabbath. I write about love because I can be cataclysmically selfish. I write about hope and healing because I have been pulled beneath the waves and thrown against the rocks. It is hard to describe the virtue of warmth if you have never been cold before.

I suck at this. This frightful wonder called life. But we can suck at it together. No one has it all figured out. No one. And no one ever will. But we can tell each other where to find the bread.

If you're feeling lonely, you're not alone. If you're envious of others' highlight reels, remember that they're not real. You don't need to achieve anything. You don't need to make any progress. You don't even need to grow. The only place you need to be is here. And you're here.

So how do we face the darkling days? Not with a redoubling of our efforts, but with a double-down on grace.

Make a practice today of grace. Extend it to yourself, and then out to others. Think of something that you need to let go of, and then give it to God.

The Fecund Fallow—questions for reflection:

1. What is the richness that can be found in slowness? How can you cultivate more fallow periods in your life?

2. Is Sabbath important to you? What are the ways in which we can create more rhythm in our routines?

3. What are the small things that save you while in the midst of the big things?

4. Are there any 'promised lands' that you're longing for that are getting in the way of you living your life in the here and now?

5. Failure is a great teacher. What are the failings that you have learned most from?

Part V

O HOLY NIGHT

'Yes, if a man lives many years, let him rejoice in them all; but let him remember the days of darkness, for they shall be many.'
—Ecclesiastes 11:8

December 21

Firmament

Slumped in the bathroom, 2am,
heart crumpling beneath the weight
of its own failures.
I know there is a mirror.
I do not want to know
what it has to say.

Walk back into the bedroom
where my daughter is sleeping.
I am a hero to her.
Through the wall I can feel the mirror sneering.
I try not to sob—it would wake her up.

I peer through the curtain,
and suddenly it feels as though
I have walked over a grave.
Orion looms vast in the sky,
unfathomable in its beyonding,
and for an eternal moment
I am inhaled by the cosmos,
falling into the terror of distance.

In the firmament I am nothing.
My failures, my successes
become absurd.

My daughter stirs and I am regrounded.

Then I try something.
Turning back to the stars
I hold up the love that I have for her.
There is a change.
Now I am the colossus,
and Orion is no giant,
and all the sky seems small,
and all the mirrors are breaking.

I try not to sob.

* * *

May you know your smallness. May you be regrounded constantly by moments of beauty. And may you know the largeness of the love in which you dwell.

December 22
Hope as planetary motion

At this time of solstice, when the sun is at its lowest, when the night is at its longest—light is at its most definitive.

Darkness does not diminish light. It amplifies it. Clarifies it. It is the boundary that gives light its shape. At night, light is en-formed. The darkness becomes a forge.

Take a small candle into the deep dark and it turns into the North Star.

O Holy Night.

Solstice marks the beginning of the Turn—the slow hemispheric shift towards warmer, longer days: hope as planetary motion.

At this time of solstice, the zenith of the dark betrays its vulnerability. It has peaked. And we are still here.

Now, it will begin to diminish. It will take time. It will be hard. Winter will not let go easily.

But it will, eventually, always, let go.

For now, we lay low. We hibernate. We curl up together in the deep furrows of the night; we let winter do its work.

At this time of solstice, at this moment of darkest dark, we can smile, knowing that the year has turned. That all things, one day, will turn.

O Holy Night.

What moments have there been in your life when the darkness has been at its zenith? When everything seemed to be going wrong? Thank God that you made it through—that you are still here. Declare that there will be other turns towards warmer days in your life.

December 23
When there is no room at the inn

All the inns were full.

It is an evocative detail, one that says more than it says. It encapsulates two related themes that repeat throughout scripture.

One: when it is time for something new to be born, it is probably not going to be in a place of comfort. It is not going to be clean. It is not going to be well-lit. It is not going to go according to plan.

Two: truth is not necessarily going to be found in the places that you might expect. Revelation rarely finds a home in systems or institutions—the cosy structures that we seek shelter in. There is no room for it there.

The divine is usually found in the margins. In the voice calling in the wilderness. In the strangers who get turned away.

God is an outcast.

The prophets are desert poets, spitting bars of thunder at the ivory towers.

The angels are drifters, roaming the darkling hills, knowing it is there that they will find the people who might understand.

All the inns were full. So don't worry if you find yourself on the outside.

Outcast God,
Help us to not despise the discomfort of new birth in our lives. Give us strength and conviction in those moments where we find ourselves on the outside. Thank you that you are there in the wilderness. Open our eyes to help us to see what might be happening in the darkling hills.
Amen.

Christmas Eve
Where the stars lead us

Astrology has been described by many Christians as being demonic. There is some classic Christian contradiction here, since at the heart of the Christmas story—which is at the heart of the faith—there is unmistakably a hefty dollop of astrology.

There is no getting around the fact that a group of people (people who in most other circumstances would be declared by the church to be 'heathens') saw a star, declared it to be portentous, and found the portent to be accurate. The birth of Christ was written in the stars.

For most of human history, and certainly in the days of the Christmas story, astrology and astronomy were one and the same thing. Until the 19th century, people had no way of knowing for certain what stars are—and mystery is fertile ground for meaning.

We now know exactly what stars are. So can we still find meaning in them?

While much of the mystery may be gone, the awe and the wonder remains. Perhaps, given what we have discovered about the vastness of the universe, that wonder has even increased. So much of what we cling tight to disintegrates amid the colossus that is the night sky.

Modern science has made us powerfully aware of just how small we are. We are not the centre of anything. We are less than a speck of dust.

The stars remind me to dethrone myself. They remind me that it is not about me. They remind me that I am nothing unless I am part of something. This is deeply counter-cultural. Society these days tells us that absolute significance is found in the self. Individualism—along with the other isms: capitalism, consumerism, materialism—is the dominant narrative of our age. The stars lead us away from that.

And then there is that one star in particular. The star of Bethlehem. The Christ-portent. And what is Christ? Selflessness. Inclusion. Interconnectedness. The great something that we are part of.

O Holy Night—questions for reflection:

1. What are the moments in your life that have humbled you? Have these been positive or negative experiences?

2. Have there been times in your life when it feels as though 'the darkness is at its zenith'—where everything seems to be going wrong? How did you get through those times, and does this change the way you look at life now?

3. 'Truth is not necessarily going to be found in the places you might expect.' Does this resonate with you? What are the moments when you have felt 'on the outside', but have found God there?

4. What does the star of Bethlehem mean to you?

Coda

THE FLESH OF THE WORLD

'The Word became flesh, and lived among us.'
—John 1:14

Christmas Day

The flesh of the world (an alternative Christmas message)

The waiting is over. The preparation and anticipation is over. Now we enjoy the fruits of Christmas.

Which are what, exactly?

Family and friends? Yes.
The birth of the new? Definitely.
The wonder of possibility? Absolutely.
Hope in the hardest of times? For sure.
Light in the darkness? Certainly.

And we know that the darkling days make this light more meaningful, not less.

Christmas is all of these things. But what if it is meant to be more? What if it is meant to completely flip the way we see the world?

The way we see the world needs flipping. Because we have a problem. And that problem is that we have entirely the wrong notion of what 'being spiritual' is.

The official definition of spiritual is 'the quality of being concerned with the human spirit or soul *as opposed to material or physical things*.' [Emphasis my own.]

Non-material. Intangible. Other-worldly.

It is the idea that the divine is somewhere else. That the physical needs to be transcended. That the reality we ought to seek is not the reality that is here, now.

It is an idea that comes to us from the ancient Greeks, rather than the ancient Hebrews. And it is an idea that the Christmas story exposes as utterly false.

The word as *flesh*. Divinity manifest in skin, blood, and bone. Heaven; here. Not as a one off, but as a reminder of an ultimate, eternal truth: flesh is good. Skin. Soil. Sunlight. Snow. Rock. Sweat. Bark. Petal. Grass. The world is good. It is good to be here.

Soul is not opposed to the material; it is part of it. God is fleshy. To be spiritual is to be physical—it is to embrace the living, present world.

Christ could not have been the light of the world without being the flesh of the world.

We cannot be the light of the world without being the flesh of the world.

To be spiritual is to eat and drink. It is to touch and to taste. It is to sing and to dance. It is to make things with our hands. To get dirt beneath our nails. It is to hug and kiss and play and walk and run and swim and hold hands and climb trees and laugh and cry— whatever it is that rings the sweet bell of your body.

It is to be here, now.

So this Christmas, may you be reminded of the goodness of you. The goodness of your flesh. The goodness of the physicality of this world.

The message from the pulpits today will be: God is with us. Well, where else would the divine be?

'The light shines in the darkness, and the darkness has not overcome it.'

—John 1:5

About the author

Gideon is a poet, environmentalist and liturgist who lives in Berkshire, England. He is at his happiest when walking up a mountain, reading books, drinking coffee in his garden, or climbing trees with his daughter. He has published two books of poetry—*Devastating Beauty* and *Rumours of Light*—has an MA in Creative Writing, and works for a global humanitarian agency.

Glory to the winters morning,
darkling yet nonetheless
eloquent of possibility

Glory to the fading year, the
falling light
heavy with ending yet
nonetheless

dropping hints of beginning.

Glory to slowness, quietude, rest,
so far from what we are
taught but nonetheless so
necessary.